Sir John Kingston James

Daydreams, to which are added some translations from the Italian

Sir John Kingston James

Daydreams, to which are added some translations from the Italian

ISBN/EAN: 9783742854858

Manufactured in Europe, USA, Canada, Australia, Japa

Cover: Foto ©Andreas Hilbeck / pixelio.de

Manufactured and distributed by brebook publishing software (www.brebook.com)

Sir John Kingston James

Daydreams, to which are added some translations from the Italian

DAY DREAMS.

DAY DREAMS,

TO WHICH ARE ADDED SOME TRANSLATIONS FROM THE ITALIAN.

BY

SIR JOHN KINGSTON JAMES, Baronet, M.A.

CORRESPONDING MEMBER OF THE ROYAL ACADEMY
DELLA CRUSCA.

Author of a Translation of Tasso's "Gerusalemme Liberata."

"She was my vision in the night,
My waking dream by day."
Old Song, 1607.

LONDON:
PRINTED FOR PRIVATE CIRCULATION.
1879.

CHISWICK PRESS:—C. WHITTINGHAM, TOOKS COURT,
CHANCERY LANE.

TO

THE ARCH-CONSUL AND MEMBERS OF

THE ROYAL ACADEMY

DELLA CRUSCA.

TO YOU I DEDICATE THESE LEAVES, AS EARNEST OF

THE DEEP AND ABIDING SENSE OF THE

GREAT HONOUR CONFERRED, IN ELECTING ME

A MEMBER OF YOUR ILLUSTRIOUS

BODY.

J. K. J.

CONTENTS.

	Page
To the Arch-Conful and Members of the Royal Academy Della Crufca	1
To Garibaldi	6
Oft at the hour when day is breaking	11
Tranflating Taffo	18
The Girl and the Bird	22
To ——	25
To C. I. J.	27
To ——	29
Ye alderliefeft Dublin hills!	31
To ——	33
To a Favourite Canary that I trod upon . .	35
Verona	38
Venice	41
Spezzia	44
To ——	46
Glengariffe	50

	Page
To G. H.	52
To the River Guul, Norway	54
To the Bride—a River	56
What is it sheds such magic o'er a name?	58
On Hearing that a Beautiful Girl was Dying	59
To ——	61
To ——	63
Cui Placet Oblivifcitur, cui Dolet Meminit	65
Adeline	67
When shall we meet again?	69
They told me I should not believe	71

Translations.

Tanto Gentile	75
Del Pellegrini	76
Voi che Afcoltate	79
Era il Giorno	81
Son Animali	83
Quanto Piu M' Avvicino	85
Solo e Penfofo	87
I'vo Piangendo	89
Se Lamentar	91
In Qual Parte del Ciel	93
Laffo che Mal Accorto	95
Io Amai Sempre	97
Io Son fi Stanco	99
Cefare Poi	101
Or che il Cielo	103
Levommi il Mio Penfier	105

Contents.

	Page
Chi Vuol Veder	107
Ne Mai Pietoso Madre	109
Erano i Capei D'oro	111
Benedetto sia 'l Giorno	113
Rotta è L'alta Colonna	115
Non Puo far Morte	117
Vago Augelletto	119
In the sweet echoes that extracted are	121
Gli Occhi di Ch'io	123
Si Spesso a Consolarmi	125
Mentre che' Amor	127
Come Creder Debb'io	129
Written on the Statue of Night	131
Poi che Sdegno	132
Lieta e Chiusa	134
Padre Eterno del Ciel	136
Parmi che'l Sol	138
Orrida Notte	140
Doglia che Vaga	142
Mormoranti	144
La Prigion Fu	146
La Bella Pargoletta	148
Diodati	149
Anch'io	151
Italia! O Italia	153
Ov' e Italia	155
O, death, that tak'st so great a part of me	157
Aura Soave	159
This mortal life, which seems so fair	161

Contents.

	Page
Ah! little bird! how very dear thou art	162
A rose Lycoris gave her flame	163
Che far Potea	164
The Last Farewell	166
Due Ninfe	168
Chi mi Vede	170
Quando la Fe	172
Donna che Bella Sia	174
Il Sogno	175
Heaven made us happy fathers desolate	176
After the ball-room's glare	178
Quando Elpin	180
Alfieri	182
Sonnet affixed to the Portal of St. Peter's, Rome	184
The lilies on Cogava's brink	186
The bird of song in Naniva	186
Where is the realm of the wind	187

TO THE ARCH-CONSUL AND MEMBERS
OF THE ROYAL ACADEMY
DELLA CRUSCA

ON BEING NOMINATED A CORRESPONDING MEMBER.

SCARCE had I hoped that in my
    waning years,
  When every sense is burden'd with
    their weight,
I should experience a new pleasure—I
That had exhausted all the old—youth, health,
Arms, idleness, ev'n every hope, save the one,
And foreign travel, and the arch delight
Of telling in our tongue an alien's thoughts.
Ev'n this, the master passion of my prime,

Began somewhat to pall, although, at times,
When musing o'er the great original,
All its old charm came back as vividly
As when at first beneath its spell I choked.
From fairest bower I pass once more to field,
Where the horrible, harmonious trumpet rings,
Then back from all its carnage and its din
To the sweet, silent solitudes of love.
Now seems the poem on a rose leaf writ,
Now on a shield amid the fume of war.
Happy, thrice happy, do I deem the choice
That led me to explore its boundless wealth,
Instead of baring my own poverty!
But still the poet ever seem'd a star
Whom I could neither grasp nor realize,
He loom'd so distant, stately, and sublime;
When, of a sudden, all amazed, I start
To find that as 'twixt heaven and earth we
    meet.
But can all this be true?—or, do I dream,
And wake to find life's dream reality—
Now that all former pleasures are eclipsed,

Hearing my humble self in the same breath
Named with Torquato Tasso—and by You!
And that your great Academy has deign'd
In me to honour the illustrious dead.
But no; I cannot ev'n in thought allow
Myself to arrogate such honour—nay,
Rather would I his mighty shade invoke,
And in the midst of you who know him best,
His pardon ask that, having dared so much,
I had not better represented him;
Having fail'd to follow his transcendent flight,
Or catch the inspiration of his muse,
Nor gave my country but a bastard sound
Of his harmonious and majestic verse,
Which after lapse of ages echoes still,
And with as grand sonorous music rings,
As when he first in his full vigour sang.
But haply, if long study and great love
Of my great master may excuse defects,
I shall not seek forgiveness all in vain,
Assured of your indulgent sympathy,
Who in my poor attempt have recognized

An honeſt wiſh to extend Italian fame,
And whoſe approval is, I feel, a ſpur
To rouſe me to freſh efforts, and at leaſt,
By them my utter gratitude to ſhow.
Not kings, though they the fount of honour deem'd,
Could have beſtow'd an honour half ſo prized
As that which from your hands I now receive
And, as firſtfruits, I crave the privilege
To atone with him[1] whoſe loving care has raiſed
A living monument to Taſſo's fame,
And on it place, in kindred ſympathy,
The wreath your favour has accorded me,
But which fits ill upon my bluſhing brow.
So for the future may a common love
Your members bind, conſtraining them to cry
With one accord, and with a ſingle voice,
"Onorate l' altiſſimo poeta!"
And ſo efface the undeſervèd ſtains
Upon him caſt by ſons of yours of yore.

[1] Signor Ceſare Guaſti, Secretary of the Academy.

Thus were rewarded the long years of toil,
Thus crown'd the afpirations of a life!
Thus could I vaunt at leaſt reflected fame,
If link'd with Taſſo's my unworthy name.

TO GARIBALDI.

Milan, October, 1860.

ONCE more I pass Alps' icy chains,
   And feel already in my veins
     The blood more light and free;
   Into new life it seems to leap
As I descend thy mountains steep—
   Enchanting Italy!

Here pregnant earth and nature teem
With rank exuberance, they seem
   Unlike our latitudes;
The very grape upon the vine,
As if anticipating wine,
   Its amber juice exudes.

And what rich contrasts strike the eye!
Oleanders 'gainst yon azure sky,
   In crimson drifts behold.
What lovely tints, what mellow tones,
The purple figs, the very stones
   Here lichen'd into gold!

Again I hear the glowing tongue
That Petrarch, Tasso, Dante, sung;
   To me, its simple sound
Appears more sweet than all the sense,
Than all the wit or eloquence
   In other language found.

But Hark! who doth his thunders launch,
Collecting as an avalanche
   Fresh force from every side?
Who, rolling onwards gathers strength
From kindred souls, aroused at length,
   Their joy, their hope, their pride!

Who came, faw, conquer'd—nay, whofe
    name
Won bloodlefs victories ere he came—
    Whofe fhadow fcared away
The ruffian hordes whom tyrant power
Had bribed with gold—but in the hour
    Of danger, where were they?

They could not fave the Bourbon's throne
From one who bearded them alone,
    And did a realm o'erthrow:
Who won their hireling ranks and took
St. Elmo's fortrefs by a look,
    Nor ftruck a fecond blow.

Since faith of all his powers was chief,
He paufed not to believe belief,
    But haften'd to the goal.
Self-truft, the child of fimple faith,
Our ftay in life, our hope in death,
    So utterly fill'd his foul.

To Garibaldi.

Like noxious vapours, which the sun
Dispels, by simply shining on,
  So at his mere advance
The King fled howling in dismay,
The motley hosts dissolved away
  At Garibaldi's glance.

To thee and to thy loyal King
The inebriate people pæans sing
  From rise to set of sun;
On Milan's dome the snowy spires
Blaze with the light of thousand fires
  That tell of freedom won.

And soon there will be heard no more
From Venice to Sicilia's shore
  The Goth's barbaric twang;
But in its place will ring the "Si"
Of one united Italy,
  As Dante dream'd and sang.

But though Utopian sophists wrote,
With giant force thy right hand smote—
   And so broke through the charm.
The poet's hope, the patriot's scheme,
Had still remain'd an idle dream
   Without thy trenchant arm.

Hence unborn ages will not fail
Thee, Garibaldi, yet to hail
   As the most glorious son
Of that fair land thy arm did free
From torture, chains, and slavery,
   Thou second Washington!

Thee we shall see, the contest o'er,
Thy sabre sheath'd, retire once more
   To lone Caprera's isle;
Despising earth's most sought-for ranks,
Content to read thy country's thanks
   In her awaken'd smile.

"He who does not imagine in stronger and better lineaments, and in stronger and better light than his perishing mortal eye can see, does not imagine at all."—BLAKE.

OFT at the hour when day is break-
    ing,
  Between a-sleeping and awaking,
    I see with still-closed eyes
Bright visions, so intensely bright
That, melting with excess of light,
    They vanish as they rise.

  Glimpses of golden lands I snatch,
  Strains of unearthly music catch,
    Borne on whose lofty flight
  I spurn the earth, and as I rise
  To heaven, it seems the opening skies
    My ravish'd soul invite.

Into the measureless expanse
Of peopled planets I advance,
   Where Jupiter and Mars,
And Mercury and many more,
Though of the brightest, pale before
   The illimitable stars.

And higher, higher, ever on,
Far past the regions of the sun,
   The ecstatic spirit springs
To new and ever-brightening spheres,
Whose music in my spell-bound ears
   With sound seraphic rings;

And thinks, as all entranced it roams,
" These stars, it must be, are the homes
   Of mortals after death—
The many mansions which the Lord
In His reveal'd life-giving Word
   To mankind promiseth."

Transported by such thoughts, I find
Two powers contending in the mind
   Which sdeigning the control
Of consciousness to bind it, feels
A something that unconscious steals
   Upon the hidden soul.

A something which we can't define,
But which, less human than divine,
   Unlocks the secret springs
Of a mysterious latent sense
That tells of future providence,
   And of forgotten things.

The ghosts of scarce-remember'd years,
And shadowy forms and shadowy fears,
   Of joys for ever fled,
Of hope that drooping oft revives,
Of faith that unextinguish'd lives,
   Though hope itself be dead.

And indefinable sensations,
Vague yearnings, struggles, aspirations—
　A doubtful second sight
That can but dimly, blindly see,
Till quicken'd from its lethargy,
　By more than mortal light.

And she, my darling upon earth,
Transfigured through the second birth,
　In radiant youth is there;
But much more beautiful she seems
Than ever in my wildest dreams
　I had imagined her.

Her hair floats on her neck, her eyes
Have caught fresh meaning from the
　　skies,
　And all beatified
An angel she before me stands,
And beckoning with uplifted hands,
　Invites me to her side.

Do I waking think, or sleeping dream?
As things past comprehension seem
  My 'wilder'd thoughts to strain,
And in their wanderings to have caught
A spark beyond the pale of thought
  That penetrates the brain,

Which inform'd with transcendent light
Revels in riotous delight
  To sober sense unknown,
Making of all that science knows,
Of all that fancy can disclose,
  An empire of its own.

By such celestial virtue fired,
Columbus saw, as if inspired,
  Another world, whence he,
In full-plumed faith his sails unfurl'd,
And reach'd that undiscover'd world
  Across an uncross'd sea.

So we may in this mortal strife
Trace shadows of that other life,
  For man by Jesus won,
But which, as will'd by Supreme will,
We shall not fully see until
  Our earthly race is run.

The shipwreck'd sailor in his hour
Of extreme peril feels a power—
  A spell—a know not what,
Which at the moment ere he sinks
Welds in one lengthen'd chain the links
  Of time and place forgot.

And as beneath the water yawns,
Before his sight a future dawns
  Of mingled doubt and dread;
A memory for life entomb'd
Is in that awful hour exhumed;
  The grave gives back its dead.

As thus the darkneſs, touch'd with light,
Lays open to his ſtartled ſight
   The long arrears of ſin;
Like one exploring haunted halls,
Whom ſudden ſpectral fright appals,
   He dares not look within.

For who will venture to gainſay,
When at the laſt doom-dealing day
   Our God our Judge we ſee,
That His dread record of the ſoul,
Be not the everlaſting roll
   Of tell-tale memory?

But, thank'd be God! in child-like faith
We can deride the power of death,
   Through Chriſt's atonement free,
And with the inſpired apoſtle ſing
Triumphant, "Where is, death, thy ſting?
   Where, grave, thy victory?"

TRANSLATING TASSO

ON THE BANKS OF THE AWBEG— SPENSER'S MULLA.

ENTRANCED for hours by Mulla's
  stream I sit,
    And on the page that once taught
      Spenser pore;
For he drank deep of Tasso's muse; from it
  He drew his love of legendary lore.

Thus both his founts of inspiration I
  Have at command—the river and the book,
While in my lap Torquato's volumes lie,
  Beneath my feet still rolls the immortal brook.

Here where the beeches overarch its stream,
  And with their shade conceal day's garish light,
Rapt in a world of waking thought I dream:
  Nor idly wait return of slow-paced night.

My sole distraction now—ah! blissful ease—
  Is from their haunts to lure the golden trout,
Where curls the water with propitious breeze,
  And drag with zest my little victims out.

Historic Mulla! like thy living stream
  May my undying numbers glide along,
And with like strength and like transparence teem,
  The flowing tide of my harmonious song.

And while pursuing its uncheck'd career,
  Still varying beauties like thyself unfold;
There stealing gently—dashing madly here,
  Deep, yet not tame, though sparkling still not cold.

Now genial May with violets gems the banks,
   And the sward robes in suit of brightest
      green ;
With wild wood-sorrel pregnant Nature pranks
   The spot still haunted by a Faery Queen.

Not from bald fancy had the poet sought
   His inspiration, had he seen as I
Her living charms with all the magic fraught
   Of thy more vivid springs—reality !

My task is light to copy, not create,
   Were words but able to portray the grace,
And catch those beams of soul that animate
   The rapt expression of her angel face.

In each whose change I seem to recognize
   The play of thought that causes it, and see
In the full meaning of her eloquent eyes
   The very soul and source of poetry.

And if I now o'er Tasso's pages throw
    A warmth, a colour, howsoever slight,
If through my pen Armida's beauties glow,
    However faintly, in his blaze of light:

Thine is the due whose loveliness and worth,
    First touch'd my heart, and raised my soul
        above
The low and sensual desires of earth,
    And gave foretaste of heaven in thy love.

Castle Widenham.

THE GIRL AND THE BIRD.

HE night had scarce her veil with-
	drawn,
And stars still mock'd the doubt-
	ful dawn,
   When up from where she lay
Sprang Mabel, heedless of the dark,
In her desire to hear the lark
   Salute the break of day.

Oft, oft she had been waken'd by,
When fast asleep, the joyous cry
   Of his familiar note:
But now awake, she sought the first
Spontaneous, passionate outburst
   Of his sleep-freshen'd throat.

The Girl and the Bird.

The vermeil tints now golden turning
Set nature's plaſtic features burning
  Beneath the ſun's fierce brow,
When, as if quicken'd by its flame,
From all the buſhes muſic came,
  A voice from every bough.

She liſtening at her lattice ſtood,
And ſaw from out the miſt-wreathed
      wood
  A thouſand ſongſters riſe;
Some flutter'd up and quick reſunied
Their perch; their pinions others plumed,
  As if to mount the ſkies.

But paſt the reſt, near out of ſight,
As ſcorning limits to his flight,
  The heavenly ſkylark ſoar'd;
And as from earth he farther flew,
More weird and more unearthly grew
  The melody he pour'd.

In unison her features play'd,
And reproduced each light and shade
　　Of his enraptured strain.
A new-born joy she seem'd to snatch,
And, as it were, the madness catch
　　Of his delirious brain.

Her frenzy heighten'd by the bird's,
Had fail'd by mere articulate words
　　To paint delight so strong.
As deep a meaning you could trace
In her expressive, eloquent face
　　As in the wild bird's song.

TO —— ——.

THE autumn leaves are falling fast,
   The wind makes melancholy
      moan
   Among the beeches rudely blown
By dank November's blast.

The sick senescence languisheth
   Of an effete expiring year,
   And faded are and grey and sere
The colours of its death,

Save where some fiery creeper shows
   In its ensanguined hectic bloom,
   The fever that foreruns its doom,
The taint that marks his close.

No more updrunken by the sun,
   But swoln with rains which now are rife,
   The streams alone have larger life,
And with more riot run.

The insects born of spring are dead,
   Nor of the birds that came with May
   Do any in our cold clime stay,
But to the south have fled.

And with them thou—while I in lone
   And bitter solitude remain,
   And champ the curb, and fret the rein
That holds me here—thou gone.

And if at times I seem more gay,
   It is the better to conceal
   The utter loneliness I feel,
But would to none betray.

TO C. I. J.

WITH A MOSAIC BROOCH OF FORGET-ME-NOTS ON HER BIRTHDAY.

HOUGH silent I, these flowers reveal
The setting current of my thought,
And utter what I utterly feel,
   Forget-me-not!

Forget-me-not as years roll by,
But let it be my happy lot,
That thou respondest to the cry,
   Forget-me-not!

I careless if remember'd now,
Or if by absent friends forgot,
My only care, my prayer that thou,
   Forget-me-not!

Living I'll ever write this day,
However diſtant be the ſpot,
And when I'm dead theſe ſtones will ſay,
>Forget-me-not!

Florence, May 6, 1860.

TO —— ——.

IS hard to tell, when looking upon thee,
    Whether thou art more good or fair or wife.
Did ever mortal move fo gracefully,
    Were ever feen fuch fympathetic eyes?
And when converfing on fome favourite theme
    Thou addeft knowledge to one's fpecial lore
Amazed one is to find the fubject teem
    With latent beauties unobferved before.
Then all thofe better works which will endure,
    When thefe extrinfic gifts have pafs'd away—

To tend the sick, the needy, and the poor,
   To love thy neighbour, and thy God obey—
All these combine to render thee what no man
Has ever seen till now—a perfect woman.

   Florence, 1878.

YE alderliefeſt Dublin hills!
   On leaving you my full heart fills,
     And fill mine eyes with tears,
  Ye conjure up a ſhadowy train
Of bygone pleaſure daſh'd with pain,
   And grave with falling years.

Ye are the ſame, but ah! how changed
Am I ſince as a boy I ranged
   Your gorſe-fringed, fragrant ſlopes,
Ere able to diſtinguiſh truth
Amid the blinding fumes of youth,
   And youth's fallacious hopes.

But now I see with other eyes,
And though the mist that on them lies
   The visual sense obscure,
Still through the insight of the mind,
No more from clouds of error blind,
   Perception is more sure.

I see the changes wrought by time
Upon green youth and golden prime,
   And feel—myself grown old—
How small the chance that on this earth,
The loving pair who gave me birth
   I shall again behold.

Still let us hope,—this short life past,—
That we shall haply meet at last,
   To part no more in heaven,
Where free from sorrow and from pain,
We shall eternal peace obtain,
   Forgiving and forgiven.

On board the " Ulster."

TO —— ——.

1876.

NOW comes that joyous feafon of the year,
 When in their emerald apparel clad,
 The woods re-echo with the wild bird's fong;
When the fifh fpring and grubs turn butter-flies,
And nature breathes forth univerfal love,
And all is hope and promife; when each flower,
Though of the fimpleft, cowflip, violet,
Or the pale primrofe, is inftinct with life
And flouts her flaunting fifters of July;
And if with many another lovely flower

You have been stricken down, God grant that you
Reap utterly the genial influence
And fullest power of vivifying May.
Its balmy breath brace up the unstrung nerves,
Fresh force impart into the drooping frame,
And graft its roses on the pallid cheek.
May grace and peace be multiplied in you!
God give you of the fatness of the earth,
And may He give you of the dew of heaven,
He who to glory calls us by His Christ.
And after that you have sufferèd awhile
Perfect you, strengthen, stablish, settle you.
And as at this boon season we behold
New life and beauty in the inanimate world,
And know that save corn die it bides alone,
But if it die it bringeth forth much fruit,
So knowing that we must pass from life to death,
May that belief confirm, increase our faith
In Him who died for us that we may live.

TO A FAVOURITE CANARY THAT I TROD UPON.

Fontainebleau, 1860.

NO found did aye so sweet appear,
  Or fall so welcome on mine ear,
    As that which now I heard.
  Ah! how my spirit did rejoice
To catch once more thy gentle voice,
    My alderliefest bird!

Since I had deem'd were ever hush'd
Those dulcet notes as almost crush'd
    Beneath my feet he lay,
Quick came and went his fluttering breath,
His eyelids closed,—alas! of death
    He seem'd the guileless prey.

But that I thought it sinful, I
Had pray'd to God thou might'st not die,
    Beloved as thou art;
On bended knee had sought in prayer
Relief against the keen despair
    That wrung me to the heart.

"Live, live, my darling little pet,
Live, live," I cried,—" nor leave me yet,
    Again thy bright eyes ope."
Mine own with blinding tears were dim
As piteously I gazed on him,
    Almost bereft of hope.

When lo! he piped—not skylark's note
When straining his mellifluous throat
    The dawn of day to greet,
Not nightingale in greenwood grove
When pouring forth his soul in love
    Was ever half so sweet.

On a Favourite Canary.

By warrior bold the clarion's ſtrain,
By thirſty traveller falling rain,
    By wave-toſt pilgrim ſhore,
By miſer piles of glittering wealth,
By patient gleams of coming health—
    Were never welcomed more.

Flutter again thy gladſome wing,
Thy top-knot ruffle,—ſing, dear, ſing,
    Thou ſhould'ſt not me refuſe,
For there are many friends on earth,
And many a thing of greater worth,
    That I would liefer loſe.

VERONA.

THE moon is up, and not a single cloud
Floats in heaven's sapphire vault—the busy world,
With all its sober, unromantic truths,
Is veil'd behind yon curtain, star-inwrought,
Which, as a drop scene on the mimic stage,
Appears to fall from heaven, and for awhile
Shut out appearance of prosaic fact.
Abstracted thus from dull realities,
Fond fancy soars upon unfetter'd wing,
And, of the present heedless, views the past
Through the rose medium wrought by poetry.

And on what spot of more poetic drift
Could she her vision ope? Here still she sees
The enamour'd Juliet, on yon balcony,
Hang o'er the music of her Romeo;
Still hears the false and fickle Proteus
Sigh as he sings, "Ah! where is Sylvia?"
While on this square, by shadows mystified,
His deathless spirit stalks. For it was here
Great Can received the greater Florentine,
And Dante's spirit makes it hallow'd ground.
For if there's aught of poor mortality
That seems to scape the common doom of death,
And still retain its old vitality,
'Tis the ethereal essence that survives
In the rapt numbers of undying song,
Which can with more religious influence,
Than mitred prelate in empurpled robe
Sublime and consecrate the meanest spot.
'Tis not, if we had power to raise the dead,
And converse hold with the illustrious past,
An Alexander or Napoleon

That we would summon from the silent grave,
But Shakespeare, Dante, or the bard who sung
Of freed Jerusalem. The warrior's fame
Were dead, not living through the poet's verse.

I must to bed—to dream, but not to sleep.

Verona, 1861.

VENICE.

AST night I had a ſtrange, unearthly
dream:
Methought I enter'd a vaſt city, where
The ſtreets were water, and I lay reclined
In an enchanted bark—nor knew I how
It floated ever onward, ſince naught ſeem'd
To give it motion in its errant courſe,
And all was ſtill and ſilent as the grave.
The glaſſy bed on which the ſhallop ſwam
Was not a river, but more like the ſea,
And dead ſave where it ſhimmer'd into life
Beneath the unclouded moon. No banks
were there,

But on each side rose up huge palaces,
Their portals level with the watery way.
Some massive piles as if by giants built,
Others light, airy structures, that appear'd
More like the weird creation of a dream.
Mysterious boats, with dusky trappings hung,
Pass'd and repass'd, from out whose sable depths
Sounds that belied their gloomy origin
Flash'd on my startled ears. Anon I saw
An open space by myriad lamps illumed,
O'er which a turret threw its stately shade.
Two sides were lined by marble palaces,
And on the third a gorgeous edifice,
Rich with barbaric gold and painted walls,
And fretted work and heaven-aspiring domes,
On countless columns based and crown'd with spires,
Loom'd indistinctly 'gainst the starry sky.
Then down a stream scarce broader than the boat,
Beneath innumerable bridges, I

Turn'd, through thick maſſes of ſuſpicious
   ſhade.
One bridge there was that tower'd above the
   reſt,
And ſpann'd two beetling blocks, on paſſing
   which
Deep ſighs and ghaſtly wailings froze my
   pulſe.
We then plunged into gloom more deep and
   denſe.
    *   *   *   *   *
Next morn I woke, and found myſelf in
   Venice.

Venice, 1861.

SPEZZIA.

OW beautiful this morn! The silver moon
   Still rides in heaven as lady paramount,
Surrounded by a galaxy of stars.
But at each moment pales her waning charms
Before the splendour of the waking sun,
Who, in a robe of saffron-tinted sheen,
Foreshows his pompous advent. Massa's
   peaks
Are still conceal'd by overhanging clouds,
Which, like a load of care, appear t'oppress
The hills' ambition with a leaden weight.
Still, still he lingers, as if loth to chase

His unobtrufive rival from her throne,
Who pale and paler every moment grows,
Looking like maiden after midnight ball.
The eaft begins to glow, and to the fouth
Light, airy cloudlets float—pink, purple, grey.
More vivid now light flafhes all around,
Vermilion now, now orange it becomes.
The Tyrrhene coast, Gorgona's ifle appear.
The clouds grow crimfon, the blue vault more
      blue,
Till in a blaze of unendurable light
Burfts forth the full effulgence of the day.

   La Spezzia, 1861.

TO —— ——.

N youth's heyday, when vivid fancy teems
   With high-wrought visions of ideal bliss,
I never imaged in my wildest dreams
   A spot so beautiful, so bright as this.

And fain would I now trace, for thy dear sake,
   The varied charms of its umbrageous shore;
Describe the calm of its translucent lake,
   Unruffled even by the fisher's oar.

To ———— ————.

Since, though to fight so fair its furface dawns,
   No erring bark its treacherous bofom
      cleaves;
For in the midft of it a whirlpool yawns,
   That fucks all down, and not a veftige
      leaves.

Yet mirror'd in its glaffy face is feen
   The fairy fretwork of Gandolpho's towers,
And mellow'd into fofter, rarer green
   Its terraced gardens and o'erhanging
      bowers.

There Palazolo's white-wall'd convent ftands,
   And o'er it topples Monte Cavo's wood,
And clofe beneath the monaftery's lands
   Th' hiftoric fite where Alba Longa ftood.

Thefe the enchantments that my mufe infpire,
   Far from the bufy world and haunts of
      men,

And yet how faint this sketch—such scenes
 require
 The painter's pencil, not the poet's pen.

I feel how powerless are words to trace
 The slightest semblance of this magic scene;
Yet time can ne'er its loveliness efface,
 Or from my heart its living memory
 wean.

And how describe the iris' violet wing,
 Or neighbouring pines that hang like clouds
 in air,
Which now with throstle's joyous music ring,
 Now echo back the nightingale's despair.

Lost mid the concert of the feather'd choir,
 Mid buzz of bees and gadding insects'
 hum,
I cannot clothe my thoughts as I desire—
 Mid nature's melody my voice is dumb.

But hark! for vespers Palazolo ringing
  From his lone cell each cowl'd Francifcan woos,
And fee, the fun, its dying glory flinging,
  Has ftill for death referved its lovelieft hues.

Think, then, if abfent and alone, I fee
  So much to fill the heart and charm the eyes,
What were the rapture if enjoy'd with thee?
  This fpot were not then earth, but Paradife.

Albano, 1861.

GLENGARIFFE.

WOOD, water, mountain, what a glorious scene !
Is that on which mine eyes tranf-
ported hang !
The bay beneath, which but a few miles off
Is lafh'd to fury by the Atlantic waves
While meeting their ungovernable furge,
Sleeps like a mountain tarn. Narciffus-like,
The emerald ifles peer in the cryftal deep,
As if to gaze on their own lovelinefs.
The fhore is fringed with birch, whofe afpen arms,
Fann'd by the breath of morn, wave trem-
blingly,

And give as 'twere a movement to the lymph,
Unruffled else. Upon the northward slope
Of yonder mount the writhen thunderbolt
Seems to have left its trace, its jaggèd course
Being outlined there in stone. Oh! what a spot
To prompt the poet or philosopher!
For ev'n the latter, tracking nature's springs,
Must seek for large discoveries in the mind.
We little know, in its unconscious flight,
The subtle part imagination plays.
What led Columbus to discover worlds?
More fancy's impulse than mechanic rule.
Here the rapt bard will meditating sigh,
To find what faint idea he can give
Of scene like this, which, though engraven deep
Upon the faithful tablet of the mind,
Yet seeks in vain a medium to convey
His sense of its weird beauty to the world.
Thou to be felt, Glengariffe, must be seen.

Glengariffe, 1860.

TO G. H.

 BLINDING blaze of summer bloom,
An odoriferous perfume,
As if on Saba's shore distill'd,
With utter light and fragrance fill'd
That garden—it was trimly kept,
And look'd as if by fairies swept.
The flowers like ball-room beauties drest,
Though of the lovely lovelieft,
Still in their rich apparel show'd
How much to art their nature owed.
I' the centre of an avenue,
Aloft a springing fountain threw

To G. H.

Fair water, in whose plashing fall
Was heard a sound most musical—
A sound expressly form'd, 'twould seem,
To make thought-laden fancy dream.
The lady of this dainty place,
Which gains from her a living grace,
Comes daily here—they say she can't
Absent herself one day from Nant.
No wonder—for I here could stay
And pass, not hours, but life away,
Where art and nature so unite
To charm the sense of smell and sight,
And nothing lacks, save certain eyes,
To make the place a Paradise.

   Llysdulas.

TO THE RIVER GUUL, NORWAY.

HOW sweet away from cities' strife,
To lead this simple, country life,
And feel no more at school,
But free from the restraints of town,
And all its cares, to wander down
The solitary Guul.

And what enchantment! rod in hand,
To fish its sparkling stream, and land
A salmon from Flask pool;
The rise—the rush—the lightning run—
The leap—the struggle—until done
He gasps beside the Guul.

To the River Guul.

Still fleeting are thefe joys, for foon
Will pafs this pleafant month of June,
   And fteal upon us Yule,
When frozen will its furface be,
And fcarce will trickle to the fea
   The once abounding Guul.

But memory of thefe calm delights,
Thefe halcyon days, thefe dreamlefs nights,
   Nor years nor clime can cool;
As at this month, fo in December,
I'll drink to thee, as I remember
   Thy fummer golden Guul.

Bogen, 1869.

TO THE BRIDE—A RIVER.

HOW happy I when at thy side,
    Beautiful Bride!
    And though not mine thou art,
    Still thou forbiddeſt not
That I ſhould haunt the hallow'd ſpot
    That ſo enthralls my heart.

'Tis true, at times thou murmureſt,
    As on thy breaſt
    I caſt my longing eyes,
And with keen expectation ſtretch
Toward thee my eager arms, to catch
    Thy beauties as they riſe.

To the Bride—A River.

Ah, yes! thrice happy 'tis to ſtray
    When lovely May
Is opening out in all her pride,
And all her ſweets perfume the air,
With one ſo innocent and fair
    As thou, belovèd Bride!

Creagh Caſtle.

WHAT is it sheds such magic o'er a name?
    And clothes the simplest with such wondrous spell?
What influence doth the wayward mind inflame,
    And makes it thus against itself rebel?

The name that once was like another, now
    Appears imbued with some resistless sway,
Or whence this sudden flush upon my brow,
    Why such emotion doth my heart betray?

Why doth my blood with such wild fever rush?
    Canst thou, Maria, tell the reason why
I never see thy name without a blush,
    I never hear it breathed without a sigh?

On Hearing that a Beautiful Girl was Dying, if not Dead, from Spasms of the Heart.

HAT! Florence ill!—I can't believe
    That she is suffering, whom
I saw but only yester eve,
    In beauty's brightest bloom.

They only try to pierce my heart
    By telling me that death
Has shot through hers an icy dart,
    That she now gasps for breath.

She in the heyday of her prime,
    The beautiful, the gay,
'Twere hard indeed before her time
    That she were snatch'd away.

Who did where all were young and fair,
    Such admiration gain?
Who moved with such a graceful air,
    Who sang like Florence Fane?

How comes it then?—perhaps the Lord
    Hath laid our idol low,
To chasten with avenging hand
    The friends that loved her so.

And retribution thus imparts
    Her havoc to atone,
That she who broke so many hearts,
    Should perish through her own.

Ballyellis.

TO —— ——.

WHY ask thee for thy photograph
    When in my heart it lies?
Heaven's brightest rays are not by
    half
  So graphic as thine eyes.

The sunbeams when transferr'd by art
    With them no sunshine bear,
The traits are like—but ah! we start,
    For life is wanting there.

Where are the lightnings of the eye,
    The dimples on the cheek;
The blushes which though silently,
    So eloquently speak?

These are the charms no art can give,
  No portraiture impart;
These, while its colours die, still live
  Undying in the heart.

TO —— ——.

O fresh and passing fair thy face is,
   So exquisite thy mien,
That in it all the several graces
   Seem haply to convene.

Art uselessly her tribute lends
   Fresh beauty to impart,
And shows how nature far transcends
   The trickery of art.

Thy presence even hate disarms,
   Thy sovran sway to prove,
As old admirers find new charms,
   And seek again thy love.

The conſtant hand outſtretch'd to thee
   By ſome rejected ſwain,
But ſhows how wrung the heart muſt be
   That pleads and pleads in vain.

If thou art falſe my doom I know,
   My hapleſs fate foreſee,
The pain I feel for others' woe
   How paſt all thought for me!

CUI PLACET OBLIVISCITUR, CUI DOLET MEMINIT.

ERE I like this grey dial-ſtone,
    To count but funny' hours,
The taſk how eaſy in this lone,
    This gloomy world of ours!

For ev'n the moments of delight,
    I number here will paſs,
As ſwift as ſwallows in their flight,
    Or breath from looking-glaſs.

The web of care exiſtence weaves,
    Will baniſh theſe from view;
And life, like autumn's yellow leaves,
    Aſſume a jaundiced hue.

The eagle walk inſtarr'd with flowers,
  The terrace crown'd with limes,
The myrtle that triumphant towers
  In ſpite of wintry rimes—

The glen of maſs, where holy men
  Were wont to offer prayer,
The haunted wood, the fairies' glen,
  As its inhabitants fair.

The ivied abbey, the old hall,
  The ruſhing river's bend,
That laves its baſe, and, more than all,
  The welcome of a friend.

All, all will fade—regrets will mar
  Remembrance of this ſpot;
Our pleaſures ne'er remember'd are,
  Our ſorrows ne'er forgot.

   Ballynatray.

ADELINE.

'TWAS in the merry month of May,
When every bloſſom looks more gay,
  And every leaf more green;
That in the woods of Inverawe,
Lord Walter for the firſt time ſaw
  Young Adeline.

Upon the taſſell'd arches ſtood
Bright pearls of rain, and all the wood
  Was ſilver'd with their ſheen,
When like a viſion of the night,
Upon his ſtartled, ſpell-bound ſight,
  Flaſh'd Adeline.

Adown a funlit, flowery glade,
At times fhe tripp'd, at times delay'd,
  Some firftling flower to glean;
But not among them all was there
A flower fo fweet, fo frefh, fo fair
    As Adeline.

They met—fhe liften'd—in her ear
He whifper'd words fhe blufh'd to hear,
  And in that fylvan fcene
They often met—they often talk'd,
But once too oft with Walter walk'd
    Loft Adeline!

The above and the two following pieces have been fet to mufic by the author.

STANZAS FOR MUSIC.

WHEN shall we meet again?—the hour
  Has clang'd from yon green-mantled tower
That parts us, Madelaine;
And as the echoes die away
They strike a chord which seems to say,
  When shall we meet again?

When shall we meet again?—Perchance
For the last time thy earnest glance
  Has pierced my aching brain,
And read the answer that despair
Imprints in living language there,
  When shall we meet again?

Few words are utter'd by the tongue,
When to its core the heart is wrung
   By agony of pain,
But now that honour bids me fly,
From out its depths efcapes the cry,
   When fhall we meet again?

The dreams of youth diffolve, and ope
Upon a dreary wafte where hope
   Is dead, and where 'tis vain
From out the paft one ray to fteal,
Or afk the future to reveal,
   When we fhall meet again.

STANZAS FOR MUSIC.

THEY told me I should not believe
 The words that Johnny spoke,
That he was given to deceive,
 And every promise broke;
They said I would repent—regret—
I do—that I cannot forget.

My mother said he was too poor
 To wed; when poverty
Show'd its gaunt visage at the door,
 That love would quickly flee;
She stopp'd my pleading by a threat—
I gave him up, but don't forget.

And often in the wakeful night,
    And in the dreamy day,
My Johnny flits before my fight:
    I cannot tear away
His image from my memory—yet
I ftrive—I ftruggle to forget.

The love implanted in my heart
    Has taken fuch deep root,
That of myfelf it forms a part,
    And bears at times fuch fruit,
That the fweet 'gainft the bitter fet,
I would not if I could, forget.

TRANSLATIONS

TANTO GENTILE.

DANTE.

SO full of grace and modesty appears
    My liege, when she another doth
       salute,
   That not an eye to gaze upon her
dares,
  And every tongue is from emotion mute.
Unmoved she hears her praise, and passes on,
   Clad in the humble garb of modest worth,
Looking a thing from heaven above come
      down,
   To show mankind a miracle on earth.
To all the world she doth so pleasing seem,
   That through the eyes enthralment gains the
      heart,

Of which who have not felt it cannot dream,
   While from her lips, more swift than Cupid's
      dart,
Seems a sweet spirit full of love to fly,
Which the soul enters and there whispers—sigh.

DEL PELLEGRINI.

DANTE.

E pilgrim guests that through our
  city stray,
 And upon things not present
  meditate,
Come ye forsooth from countries far away,
 As your appearances would indicate?
Since as ye pass along her streets, no tear
 Falls o'er the dolorous city from your eye,
Nor do ye, heedless, in the least appear
 To comprehend her grief's intensity.
Could ye but stay to hear the tale, my heart
 Assures me with an answering sigh, that none

Would without weeping from her walls depart,
   Since from her, her own Beatrice is gone;
To tell whofe merit in the fainteft guife
Would as from ours draw tears from others'
   eyes.

VOI CHE ASCOLTATE.

PETRARCA.

 YE that hear in these my scatter'd rhymes
The mournful sighs with which I fed my heart
In the early season of my youthful crimes,
When other than from what I'm now in part;
Not only pardon do I hope to obtain,
But ruth from those that love by suffering know;
If in a style so varied I complain
Of wild delusions and insensate woe.

For now I see that to the world my name
    Has been a byword and a mockery,
Whence for myself I blush and feel deep shame,
    The bitter fruit of my idolatry,
With that clear knowledge through which now I deem
That the world's joys are but a short-lived dream.

ERA IL GIORNO.

IT was that day on which the sun
    grows black,
  As if to mourn its Maker, that
    I found
Myself, fair lady, taken all aback
  By thy bright eyes, and in their trammels
    bound.
Ill suited seem'd the occasion for defence
  Against love's cruel and insidious blows,
So that I walk'd without suspicion, whence
  My sadness for the common grief arose.
Love found me undefended 'gainst his spears,
  And saw a pathway open to the heart

Through eyes become an outlet but for tears;
  Still 'twas no honour, as I deem, to dart
Shafts againſt one unarmed, nor ev'n to ſhow,
Armed as he was from head to foot, his bow.

SON ANIMALI.

PETRARCA.

SOME animals there are of such
    strong sight,
  That the sun's noontide splen-
    dour they can bear;
Some blinded are by its excessive light,
  Nor to go forth, except at evening, dare.
Others there are whose foolish wishes turn
  Them towards the sun, because that it doth
    shine,
Who find it also has the power to burn.
  The latter case, alas! resembles mine;
For I'm not strong enough to endure the
    blaze

Of that fair sun,—my liege,—nor know I how
In darksome places to escape its rays,
  Since through these wet weak eyes, O Fortune! thou
Lead'st me to see the goal of my desire;
Thus I pursue what sets my soul on fire.

QUANTO PIU M' AVVICINO.

PETRARCA.

AS nearer I approach the final day
    That makes man's misery of brief
        duration,
    More swiftly I behold time pass
away,
And that my trust in it is vain vexation.
Not long methinks shall I be led astray
    By love, since fleeter than fresh-fallèn snow
Dissolves this heavy load of cumbrous clay,
    Through which we have a respite from our
        woe.
With death will those infensate hopes expire
    That caused me, mad-like, for so long to rave,

And fears and laughter, and laments and ire;
   And then a clearer infight we fhall have,
How oft by paths uncertain we advance,
How oft repine and figh through ignorance.

SOLO E PENSOSO.

PETRARCA.

ALONE and penſive through the
    fields I go,
    The deſert fields, with ſlow and
    meaſured pace,
Mine eyes intent to ſhun the paths that ſhow
    Of man's propinquity the ſlighteſt trace :
No other means are left me in this need
    To ſcape the ſharp obſervance of my kin,
Who in theſe joyleſs lineaments can read
    By my exterior how I burn within.
So that I fancy every hill and field
    And wood and river know the hapleſs ſtate

Of this my life, that is from man conceal'd.
   Still track I cannot find ſo deſolate,
But that Love ever at my ſide doth ſkim
With me converſing, as I do with him.

I'VO PIANGENDO.

PETRARCA.

MOURN, I mourn, the bygone years that I
   In loving thing of mortal mould have spent;
Pinions I had, yet used them not to fly,
   To crawl ignobly on the ground content.
O King of heaven! eterne, invisible,
   Which seest my wickedness, do not deny
To guide my erring thoughts when they rebel,
   And their defect with heavenly grace supply,
That if I've lived in tempest and in strife,
   I may in harbour and in quiet die;

That glorious be the ending of my life,
    If its career was vain; and, ah! be nigh
To cheer what little yet remains to me.
Thou knowest well—I hope alone in Thee!

SE LAMENTAR.

PETRARCA.

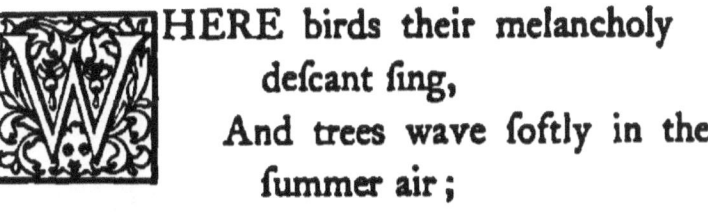HERE birds their melancholy
　　　defcant fing,
　　And trees wave foftly in the
　　　fummer air;
Where lucid water ripples murmuring—
　Heard from a frefh and flowery margent,
　　where
I of love thinking, may fit down and write;
　I fee, I hear, and underftand her whom
Heaven fhow'd but earth conceals : ev'n from
　　　that height
　Her fweet voice anfwers mine—" Ah ! why
　　confume

Thyfelf before thy time?" fhe foftly cries.
"Why for the dead indulge a living flame,
Why pour a dolorous river from thine eyes?
  Weep not for me, dear friend, my days became
Dying, eterne—and in eternal light,
When mine eyes feem'd to clofe, they gain'd new fight."

IN QUAL PARTE DEL CIEL.

PETRARCA.

WHERE in the heavens or in what
    form below
  Was found the idea from which
    Nature took
That lovely face in which she wish'd to show
  On earth the glimpse of a celestial look:
Tresses of gold so exquisitely fine,
  What goddess ever freed to summer's breath?
When did one heart such excellence combine,
  Although the prime one's guilty of my
    death?
In vain he seeks for angel loveliness,
  Who has not seen with what seductive lure

She turns her eloquent eyes; nor can he guefs
 How love is able both to kill and cure,
Who knows not with what fweet fighs fhe
 beguiles,
And how fhe fweetly fpeaks and fweetly fmiles!

LASSO CHE MAL ACCORTO.

PETRARCA.

LAS! how unconscious was I when love's flame
    First fear'd my bosom in that fatal hour,
And by degrees the tyrant lord became
    Of this my life, with full and sovran power.
I little deem'd with what persistent art
    It was enabled to pierce through, at length,
The stubborn firmness of my harden'd heart.
    But so fall those who overrate their strength.
Henceforth I know all remedy is vain,
    Other than this, my last resource, to essay

If love will heed to man's entreaties deign;
 But prayers are vain, nor will I idly pray
That my heart may more meaſuredly reſpire,
But that ſhe feel ſome portion of its fire.

IO AMAI SEMPRE.

PETRARCA.

EVER loved—nor yet from love
  forbear;
 Nay, I will love from day to day
  ſtill more,
That ſweet, ſweet ſpot where weeping I repair,
 Oft as love ravages my love-ſick core.
And I'm reſolved to love the time, the hour
 That all low thoughts within me has ſubdued,
And her the moſt whoſe angel face had power
 To win me by example to do good.
But who could thoſe dear foes, from every part,
 (Foes whom I cheriſh), aye expect to ſee

Together banded to affail my heart!
  Ah! with what forces, Love, thou conquereft
    me.
Yes—did not hope keep pace with my defire,
When I moft wifh to live, I fhould expire.

IO SON SI STANCO.

PETRARCA.

SO burden'd with the old accustom'd load
   Of vicious habits and of sin am I,
   That I fear greatly fainting on the road,
And falling captive to the enemy.
There came to save me a great friend,—'tis true,
   With utter kindness, who did not remain;
Since from my sight, scarce seen, away he flew,
   And though I strive to see him, it is vain.
But still his voice re-echoes in mine ear:
   O ye that travail, come, come unto me,

If others cloſe it not, the way is clear.
What love, what favour, or what deſtiny
Will furniſh me with wings, that, as a dove,
I may quit earth, and ſeek repoſe above?

CESARE POI.

PETRARCA.

CESAR, what time the Egyptian traitor made
    Him prefent of his foeman's honour'd head,
To mafk the joy that o'er his features play'd,
    Diffembling, wept aloud,—as it is faid.
And Hannibal, when he beheld how Fate
    Againft the forely-ftricken empire turn'd,
His grim refentment to alleviate
    Laugh'd 'mid the maffes that around him mourn'd.
Thus does it happen that the mind conceals

Its every passion under false disguise,
And ever opposite to what it feels.

Hence if at times I sing or smile, it is
Simply because I know no other way
To hide the anguish I would not betray.

OR CHE IL CIELO.

PETRARCA.

NOW that the birds and beasts deep
    slumbering are,
  That winds are hush'd, and still
    the earth and sky,
That round the heavens, Night wheels her
  silver car,
  And in their bed the wavelefs waters lie,—
I watch, I think, I burn, I weep,—for still
  Before me stands the undoer of my peace.
My life's a war, nor does my poignant ill,
  Save when I think of my destroyer, cease.
Thus from one clear and living fountain spring

The sweets and bitters upon which I feed;
One hand there is that doth while healing sting,
  Hence martyrdoms to martyrdoms succeed.
A thousand times each day, I live, I die,
So far removed from a sound state am I.

LEVOMMI IL MIO PENSIER.

PETRARCA.

Y thoughts exalted me to regions where
   She is I feek on earth, but find no more,
And high in heaven, I beheld her,—fair,
   Much fairer, but lefs haughty than before.
Taking my hand, fhe whifper'd, "In this fphere,
   My wifhes granted, thou wilt join me yet;
I am fhe who troubled fo thy life's career,
   And pafs'd my day before its fun had fet.
My blifs can't be conceived by mortal mind,
   I wait but thee, and what thou lovedft fo,

My beauteous form, which is in earth inshrined."
   Why ceafe—why ope her hand, and let me
      go?
Since by thofe chafte, compaffionate accents
      fway'd,
But little wanted that in heaven I ftay'd.

CHI VUOL VEDER.

PETRARCA.

WHO would behold what Nature can devife
   And Heaven create, fhould her contemplate who
Alone's a fun,—not folely in mine eyes,
   But in the purblind world's unheeding view.
Let him come foon, fince Death firft fteals the beft,
   And fuffers the moft criminal to ftay,
And this fair thing, expected by the bleft,
   Remains not here, but, mortal, flits away.
Here, if in time, he will each virtue fee,

Habits moſt noble, beauty exquiſite,
Knit in one frame with wondrous harmony.
Then that I'm blinded from exceſs of light,
And that my⋅verſe is voiceleſs, he will ſay,
But will for ever weep, if he delay.

NE MAI PIETOSA MADRE.

PETRARCA.

O her dear child, affectionate mother ne'er,
   Ne'er to her darling huſband, loving wife,
Gave with ſuch tender, ſuch ſolicitous care,
   Counſel ſo faithful in the ſtraits of life
As unto me that angel, who above,
   Beholding my ſad exile here below,
Oft turns upon me her old look of love,
   Fraught with a twofold ſympathy, as now
She with a mother's honeſt warmth doth fear,
   Now with a lover's burns,—then ſpeaking ſhows

What things to fhun, and what to follow here;
   Recounts our life's viciffitudes and woes,
Then prays I foon may join her 'mid the bleft,
Alone fhe fpeaking, have I peace or reft.

ERANO I CAPEI D'ORO.

PETRARCA.

LOOSE were her golden tresses in the air,
   Which toss'd them in disorder infinite,
And from her lustrous eyes, now seen so rare,
A radiance shone beyond all measure bright.
Her face (I know not if it truth express'd)
Flush'd with compassionate regard became,
Then with such amorous touchwood in my breast
What marvel that I burst forth into flame?
Not as a mortal's did her gait appear,
No,—'twas an angel that I gazed upon;

An angel's voice, too, 'twas that rapt mine ear,
A heavenly fpirit, a quick, living fun,
Was fhe I faw,—if fhe be not fo now,
The wound ftill galls, although relax'd's the
    bow.

BENEDETTO SIA 'L GIORNO.

PETRARCA.

LEST be the year, the month, the very day,
   The time, the season, the auspicious hour,
The land, the spot, where I first felt the sway
Of two bright eyes that bound me in their power.
Blest be the first delicious tender woe
When smit by Love I felt his poignant dart;
Blest be the fatal arrows and the bow,
And the sweet wounds that pierced me to the heart;
Blest the unnumber'd fair accounts that I,

Calling my liege by name, have spread around;
Bleft be the longing wifh, the tear, the figh,
Bleft every page in which fhe lives renown'd
Through this my pen,—bleft every thought and care
Which are but hers, in which none others fhare.

ROTTA È L'ALTA COLONNA.

PETRARCA.

FALLEN is the column and the laurel tree
   Whoſe kindly ſhade refreſh'd me when oppreſt,
Loſt have I what I dare not hope to ſee
   In north and ſouth, in fartheſt eaſt or weſt.
Through death a double treaſure I deplore
   That made me happy, confident, and bold,
Which neither earth nor empire can reſtore,
   Nor Oriental gem, nor power of gold.
But if this be the ſettled will of fate,
   What can I more in my affliction do

Than downcast look, with eyes for ever wet?
  O life, which art so beautiful to view!
How easily in one morning disappears
The fruit acquired by moil of many years.

NON PUO FAR MORTE.

PETRARCA.

DEATH cannot make her faireſt face unfair,
    But her fair face can lend a charm to death.
What need have I of other guidance there
    Than what her own example furniſheth?
And He who was not miſer of His blood,
    And with bold foot burſt through the gates of hell,
Seems by His dying to prove death a good.
    Come then, O death! I like thy coming well,
And do not tarry, for the time has come,
    Though not in faƈt,—it really arrived

The hour my lady left her earthly home,
   Since which a single day I have not lived;
So bound in her's my life was, that my day
Was turn'd to night when Laura pass'd away.

VAGO AUGELLETTO.

PETRARCA.

EAR little bird, that pourest forth
    thy song,
  Or weepest mournfully time
    pass'd away,
Seeing that night and winter are so long,
  And all so distant the delights of May.
If, as thou feelest thy own misery
  Thou knew'st how similar my sufferings were,
Thou wouldst to this disconsolate bosom fly,
  The dolorous anguish of my heart to share.
I know not if our lots are like, since she
  Thou mournest, it may be, is still alive,

A fate begrudged by Heaven and Death to me.
But now the season and sad hour revive
Remembrance of those sweet and bitter years,
And bid me seek thy sympathy with tears.

IN the sweet echoes that extracted are
  By thy swift fingers from the trembling chords,
Thou tell'st of love in language clearer far
  Than were attainable by subtlest words.
Before such sounds all dolorous visions flee,
  Like shades before the sun, and as I still
Imbibe the magic of such melody,
  Lost in enthralment is the force of will.
In itself perfect every note appears,
  With a new spirit of love's power replete,

When touch'd by thy dear hand—as mountain airs
  Are fill'd with fragrance fresher and more sweet,
If at morn straying through some odorous bower
They brush the uncover'd petal of a flower.

GLI OCCHI DI CH'IO.

PETRARCA.

THE eyes of which I once so fondly sung,
    The arms, the hands, the feet, the lovely face
That me so wholly from myself have wrung,
    And made so unlike others of my race.
The wavy tresses of pure, lucent gold,
    The flash of that angelic smile, which made
Of earth a paradise, have now to cold
    Unsentient, immaterial dust decay'd.
And yet I live,—and, groping in the dark,
    Lament that light beloved so much, so long,

The tempest raging, pilotless my bark;
   Then hush'd for ever be my love-plumed
      song :
Spent is the fire that erst so fiercely burn'd,
And into mourning is my music turn'd.

SI SPESSO A CONSOLARMI.

SANAZZARO.

WEET sleep returns to comfort me
    so oft
      That almost I begin to wish for
        death,
Which is, perchance, more pleasing and more
    soft,
  And sweeter, too, than man imagineth;
For if the mind can understand and see
    When the dull limbs are languishing and
      dead,
And that more comforted I seem to be
    When from the body waking thought has
      fled,

Not vain my hope that when my foul at laſt
   Has burſt the bond of her terreſtrial chain,
She wake and fee and her own pleaſures taſte.
   Rejoice then, foul, though vex'd by pre-
      ſent pain,
Since if on earth ſuch joy to thee is given,
What bliſs will thine be in thy native heaven!

MENTRE CHE' AMOR.

SANNAZARO.

WHILE love with fair ingenuous deceit,
  In its first fond delusions nursed my heart,
My mind, in verse compassionate and sweet,
  Sought its sad tale of suffering to impart;
But when from year to year increased the stings,
  And from their lofty height the flowers fell down,
Driven from those sweet sublime imaginings,
  Back on itself the conscious mind was thrown;
Hence the short course of mortal life I spend
  In lengthen'd silence and in utter shade,

Nor care for fame or other worldly end.
    Then, lady, feek fome better, worthier aid,
A fafer guide difcover with thy wit,
    For I am worn, and wafted, and unfit.

COME CREDER DEBB'IO.

ARIOSTO.

OW can I deem, O Lord, that Thou wilt hear
My cold and lifeless prayers, if while the voice
Cry for deliverance, Thou beholdest clear
How in my bondage I at heart rejoice?
Do Thou who know'st the truth deliver me,
Though my mad passions would the boon deny,
And, ah! send down Thy favour speedily,
Before I am doom'd a death of sin to die.
Pardon my many sins, O Lord eterne,
And the foul habits which so blind mine eyes

That they can scarcely good from ill discern.

To spare the penitent, man's province is,
But Thou, O Lord, alone canst drag from hell
Those who, lip-praying, still at heart rebel.

WRITTEN ON THE STATUE OF NIGHT,

BY MICHAEL ANGELO.

WROUGHT by an angel in this maſſy
    ſtone
    Is Night, which in ſuch graceful
    poſe you ſee,
And, ſince ſhe ſleeps, has life, as here is ſhown :
If doubtful, wake her,—ſhe will ſpeak to thee.

*Michael Angelo imperſonating the
    ſtatue replies :*

Sweet is my ſleep, ſtill more of ſtone to be ;
    While ſhame and ſuffering exiſt below,
Thrice bleſt am I that cannot feel or ſee,
    So wake me not,—I prythee whiſper low.

POI CHE SDEGNO.

TRISSINO.

SINCE scorn has now unriveted the chain
   That Beauty forged and Love insidious wound,
And that comes back my liberty again
   From her whose hand the links too tightly bound;
To its true good my spirit would return,
   By madness erewhile driven for a thought
That caused within my wayward heart to burn
   Ill-founded hopes, and pleasures which are naught.

Poi che Sdegno.

That led by impulse of more holy birth,
 I may perchance at that fair path arrive
Which disunites us from all thoughts of earth.
 And reason which in me was scarce alive,
But in another's impure keeping lay,
May take the reins and o'er the senses sway.

LIETA E CHIUSA.

BEMBO.

E sweet secluded haunts to which I
fly,
  Well pleased to shun the world
    and live alone,
Who grudges me amid your shade to lie,
  Now that so fervent the sun's rays have
    grown?
Seldom 'mid you I feel or grief or ire,
  And ne'er so oft is fixed on heaven my sight,
Not elsewhere do my studies so inspire
  Me with the wish to reach a higher flight.
The sweets of solitude ye taught to me,
  From you I first learn'd how surpassing sweet

It is to feel from care and croffes free.
 O ftream beloved! O well beloved retreat!
Would I could change this fea and efplanade
For your cool waters and refrefhing fhade.

PADRE ETERNO DEL CIEL.

VITTORIA COLONNA.

TERNAL Father, with what grace, what love,
   What light, what varied kindnefs doft Thou free
Man from the world and from himfelf, and move
   His heart, that freely it return to Thee;
Return'd, thou warm'ft it with Thy quick'ning breath,
   And doft with knots the moft tenacious bind,
And clencheft it with fuch ftrong nails, that death
   Appears a living honour to the mind.

Thoughts such as these a steadfast faith inspire,
   Through which is light, and through light hope reveal'd,
And hope gives life to still sublimer fire,
   Whence to the soul the fleshly passions yield,
Rebel no more,—nay, both together fly,
Of mortal cares disdainful, to the sky.

PARMI CHE'L SOL.

VITTORIA COLONNA.

HE sun, methinks, his wonted light denies,
   Less brilliant, too, his sister's glories are,
I see not wheeling through the ornate skies
   Or friendly planet or resplendent star.
A heart with valour arm'd no more I see,
   Fled is true honour, glory fair is fled,
And their companions, truth and chivalry.
   The trees are leafless and the flowrets dead,
Alone I see wild waters and black air,
   The wind refreshment gives not, nor fire heat,

Parmi che'l Sol.   139

All things on earth a different aspect wear
   Since Death my sun took to his dark retreat.
The course of nature in disorder lies,
Or truth is veil'd by sorrow from mine eyes.

ORRIDA NOTTE.

L. TANSILLO.

 HIDEOUS night, whose sable locks unbound,
　　Beneath a veil of teeming darkness lie,
Come forth from thy dark caverns underground,
　　And Nature's face in thy black colours dye.
I who have fretted at thy cold delay,
　　Not less than from the fever I endure,
How I would praise thee if thou wouldst but stay,
　　And me some sleep, ev'n for one night, procure!

I'd say that thou cam'st down from heaven,
    that thou
  Hadst myriad star-inwoven crowns, whose
      light
Adorns the world; that to the wearied brow
  Thou gavest rest, contentment, and delight.
In short, so many fair things I would say
That of sheer envy would expire the day.

DOGLIA CHE VAGA.

G. DELLA CASA.

O that diſtreſs which woman brings the heart,
   When wounding it with her empiercing eyes,
No balm can Ida's dittany impart,
   Nor lengthen'd weeping, nor deſpairing cries.
Fly then from love,—they beſt refiſt love's wiles
   Who run leaſt riſk in the unequal war;
When lovely woman ſweetly ſpeaks and ſmiles,
   Laments are preſent, death itſelf not far.
For with one look fair woman, when ſhe wills,
   Can lure the eye and rive the heart in twain.

Ah! monstrous poison, that in pleasing kills,
   Who knows of antidote to such a bane!
Ah, no! the sole correctives we possess
'Gainst love, are absence and forgetfulness.

MORMORANTI.

E. DI VALVASONE.

FRESH, hiſtoric murmuring river,
    Clearer than any cryſtal, and
    more pure,
May Heaven for ever love you, and for ever
From the fierce dog-ſtar and his rage ſecure.
On you, now ruſhing lifelike through theſe rocks,
    Ah, may no tempeſt fall, no harm deſcend;
May you unſullied or by ſwain or flocks,
    From adverſe fate, benignant Heaven defend.
May your fair Naiads' loves meet happy end,
    May both your banks unfading verdure wear,

And every feafon fome frefh beauty lend
  To your tranflucent waters. Only bear
My image, whofe reflection they have caught,
  To her who tempers and controls my thought.

LA PRIGION FU.

F. COPPETTA.

O fair the tomb was where the soul was laid
 And did so forcibly the eyesight win,
That to regard the outside others stay'd,
 Regardless of the beauties hid within.
But since with winter disappear'd the rose,
 Since now the light of those bright eyes is seal'd,
The spirit with refreshen'd vigour shows
 A thousand treasures hitherto conceal'd.
There modesty and courtesy have place,
 Of other virtues, too, the sacred quire

That man endows with fortitude and grace.
  Blind muſt they be who ſee and not admire.
Ah! bleſt am I who, ſeeing this, far more
Than erſt I loved the body, now the ſoul
  adore.

LA BELLA PARGOLETTA.

TORQUATO TASSO.

HE girl who in her youth's firſt flower
   Has ne'er felt love within her heart,
Nor heard from others of his power,
   Still with her lovely eyes will dart,
And all unconſcious ſmile,
   Nor knows what arms ſhe has the while.
Say, then, what fault with her be found,
   If men fall victims to thoſe arms
She never knew would wound?
   Oh, innocent and homicidal charms,
'Tis time that you by love were ſhown
What pain we ſuffer, in your own.

DIODATI.

MILTON.

I TELL thee, Diodati, with surprise,
   That I who erstwhile ridiculed
       the thought
   Of love, and did its stratagems
despise,
Am in its toils, like many another, caught.
Still, 'tis not vermeil cheek nor golden hair
   That dazzles me, or to whose charms I bow;
No—'tis the beauty of the heart, most rare,
   A dignified deportment, and a brow
That with the light of lovely darkness shines,
   Discourse enrich'd with language more than
       one,

And songs that from her star-encircled shrines
    Enabled were to draw the labouring moon,
And eyes, in which a fire so eloquent glows
That of small use 'twould be the ears to close.

ANCH'IO.

MAGGI.

TOO when spring ran riot in my
    veins,
  Vaunted love's fever, which con-
    sumed me long,
And, telling to the muse my darling pains,
  Made of my bitter plaints a honied song.
But now that sober manhood shows to me
  The senseless folly of my youthful years,
And that more clearly their deceit I see,
  My singing is converted into tears.
Repentance thus has led me to lament,
  And if youth's rapture was alloy'd with ills

My heart has now grown tranquil and content,
    Since sorrow vivifies, while pleasure kills.
As mad enjoyments, though so brief, destroy,
So sage affliction leads to lasting joy.

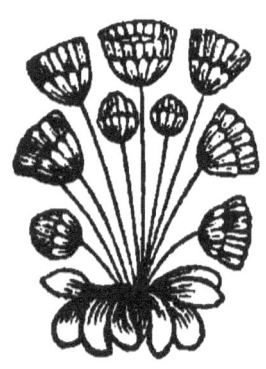

ITALIA! O ITALIA.

FILICAJA.

ITALY! O Italy! to whom
    Fate moſt diſaſtrous beauty gave, whence thou
    Infinite ills inheriteſt; thy doom
Thou beareſt branded on thy ſorrowing brow.
Ah! hadſt thou been more ſtrong, or even leſs fair,
    Then would they fear thee more or love thee leſs
Who by thy beauty ſeem conſumed, yet dare
    Challenge to death the idol they careſs.
Then from the Alps I had not ſeen a flood
    Of ſoldiers ſweep, or Gallic ſteeds daſh down

And drink, the Po encarnadined with blood;
  Nor seen thee, girt with weapons not thine own,
Aid at the hands of alien peoples crave,
Victor or vanquish'd, still for ever slave!

OV' E ITALIA.

FILICAJA.

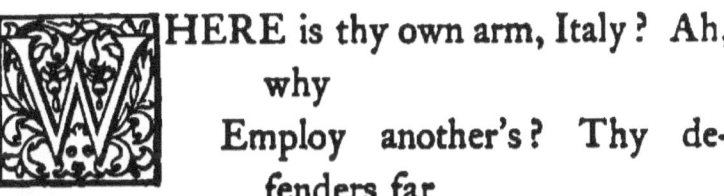HERE is thy own arm, Italy? Ah, why
    Employ another's? Thy defenders far
Surpaſs thy offenders in ferocity;
    Both were thy ſlaves, both now thy foemen are.
Iſ't thus thou keep'ſt the honour? is it thus
    Thou wouldſt the glorious empire's fame preſerve?
Thus towards that valour which was pledged to us,
    Our fathers' valour, thou wouldſt faith obſerve?

Away,—thy ancient strength repudiate;
   Go,—sleep and listless indolence espouse,
'Mid blood, groans, shrieks, and perils still more
      great.
   Sleep, vile Adulteress! till the falchion rouse
Thee from thy torpor, and, exposed thy charms,
Thee slay besotted in thy lover's arms.

FILICAJA.

DEATH, that tak'ſt ſo great a part
of me,
And leav'ſt the other outſide thy
domain,
If what love is was ever felt by thee,
Or take this too, or give that back again.
But if thy ſway ſo far extendeth not,
Me with thy native ice at leaſt endow,
And 'gainſt the blows of my unhappy lot
Thou who offendedſt ſo, defend me now.
For neither power of herbs, nor magic art,
Nor reaſon's balm ſuffice to numb the
pain,

Or close the wounds of my afflicted heart,
　Whence to my natural sorrow giving rein,
Weep, weep, I must, and try my grief to assuage
By tracing her fair image on this page.

AURA SOAVE.

MOZZARELLO.

SOFT breeze that toyeſt ſweetly with
    the air,
  And, wantoning amid the ſhrubs
    and flowers,
Firſt gathereſt the odours which they bear,
  And then diffuſeſt them in fragrant ſhowers:
O verdant meadow! O fair ruſhing ſtream,
  Retreat moſt grateful to my amorous fire,
That oft haſt liſten'd to the love-ſick theme
  Of hopes, and fears, and feveriſh deſire.
Henceforth thoſe ſounds ſo often heard by
    you
  I to an end, a very end would bring,

And much can will when ruled by reaſon do.
　　Still, if of her no more I weep or ſing,
It cannot be I ever ſhall forget
This verdant meadow and this rivulet.

GUARINI.

HIS mortal life, which seems so fair,
   Is like a feather tempest-tost,
   That favouring currents upward
     bear,
   But which is in a moment lost.
Still if at times from earth it spring
   In daring and adventurous flight,
And floats in air on outpoised wing,
   It is because its nature's light.
But soon in thousand twists and turns
To earth, since being of earth, returns.

GUARINI.

H, little bird! how very dear thou art,
 And how resembleſt thy own ſuffering
To the ſad ſtate of my enamour'd heart:
 Both captives are, and as thou ſing'ſt I ſing.
Thou ſing'ſt to her whoſe charms have ſmitten thee,
 So, with this moſt unfortunate difference, I
Sing, but to drown the pangs of memory;
 In ſong thou liveſt, while I ſinging die.

GUARINI.

A ROSE Lycoris gave her flame,
    A rose, methought, in Eden rear'd,
    And giving it so red became
That she herself a rose appear'd.
"Ah!" falter'd Batto, with a sigh
    That did his heartfelt love disclose,
"Unworthy, darling girl, am I
    To keep as gift the giving rose?"

Love, laughing, taunted rose-crown'd May:
    "How soon your flowers' sweet summer closes!"
But the fair Season answer'd:—"Say,
    Last your joys longer than my roses?"

CHE FAR POTEA.

ZAPPI.

WHAT by herself could the ill-fated bride
    Of Collatino in such danger do?
    She wept,—she pray'd,—entreaties vainly tried,
Vain were the tears that did her cheeks bedew.
Like falcon hanging o'er a dove, the sword
    In menace o'er her ivory bosom flew,
But with none help or counsel to afford,
    What could the lonely, ill-starr'd woman do?
She should have died before she sinned, we know,
    But in herself how sinn'd the fair, what time

She with her life's-blood ſtain'd the dagger?
    —No;
Alone Tarquinio perpetrated crime,
Againſt—not with her. She was guilty too,
    But only when her guiltleſs ſelf ſhe ſlew.

THE LAST FAREWELL.

ZAPPI.

DEEP in my mind that night doth memory keep
   When home I left, and left my Mary there,
That dark, difaſtrous night.—I faw her weep,
  Never leſs proud ſhe was, nor aye more fair.
Oft, oft we ſaid "Farewell," again, "Farewell,"
   And where 'twas planted, there the foot remain'd;
Oft, oft we parted, but the foot ſtill fell
  On the ſame ſpot, although to part we feign'd.
The night at length is paſt, the day appears,
  When in my extreme agony I ſaid,—

But what said I, if floods of bitter tears
   All utterance choked ? I left, by blind fate
      sped ;
But how left I ?—I cannot well aver,
   I only know I am no more with her.

DUE NINFE.

ZAPPI.

TWO maidens rivals were, in face and speech,
　In power of song, in motion, in repose;
And lovely so that near the other each
　Star with a star appear'd, twin rose with rose.
'Twere hard to say if this or that could bear
　The palm of beauty from her rival—you
Could truly say none other is so fair,
　But could not name the fairest of these two.
If such a couple had appear'd before
　The Idan shepherd, not Cythæra's queen
In charm of face had gain'd the victory o'er

This peerlefs pair. Which, then, had conqueror been?
Either the apple Paris had divided,
Or the great conteft were ftill undecided.

CHI MI VEDE.

S. MAFFEI.

E that beholds me with wan countenance
  Walk through this foreſt ſlowly and alone,
And how from time to time, as in a trance,
  I rooted ſtand, like one transform'd to ſtone;
How oft I plunge into the blindeſt ways,
  The moſt impervious and the moſt profound;
How oft mine eyes that ſtream with tears I raiſe
  Up to the ſky, then caſt them on the ground:
"Ah! in what poignant anguiſh," he would ſay,
  "In what afflićtion is that wretched man,

Who seems at times to breathe his soul away."
 Fool! thou but little knowest how love can
The senses steal, and sighs with sweets alloy;
I would not give my tears for all thy joy.

QUANDO LA FE.

CASAREGI.

WHEN my thoughts, plumed with faith from sphere to sphere
    Soar beyond heaven, O Lord, before my sight
Thou dost amid Thy wingèd choirs appear
    Within Thine own incomprehensible light.
And if from thence to my own primal night
    I turn with only reason for my guide,
All tells of Thee and of Thy Image bright,
    Which ev'n on earth in man is testified;
I see Thy Spirit, which infuses power
    In earth's huge mass, and causes life to spring

Within the grafs, the leaf, the fruit, the flower.
I fee Thee, borne on gentle breezes, wing
Thy way through air and water—yea, Thou art
Seen in all places fave my finful heart.

DONNA CHE BELLA SIA.

BONDI.

OMAN that lovely is, nor steals
   Her charms from artificial aid;
   With docile mind, a heart that feels,
And manners sweet and nobly bred.
Not quick to love, or to be won,
   Whose sense and modesty despise—
Constant and true, content with one—
   Ev'n to seem fair in others' eyes.
"Find, piteous god," to Love I said,
   "Find me that girl, where'er she be;
For I would love her,—nay, would wed."
   "If thou canst love aught else," cried he,
"Renounce thy plan, for such I ween
Was ne'er in my dominion seen."

IL SOGNO.

METASTASIO.

SHE whose love my life endears,
 In sleep, at least, sometimes appears,
  To assuage my heart's sad ache.
 Ah, love! if fair and just thou art,
To these sweet dreams more truth impart,
 Or never let me wake.

VITORELLI.

EAVEN made us happy fathers desolate,
    Taking our daughters, modest, wise, and fair.
For seeing each worthy of a nobler fate,
    Heaven summon'd both from our paternal care.
From Hymen's brightly blazing torches, mine
    Death hurried to an early sepulchre
Within a convent's seal'd enclosure, thine
    Hath given herself eternal prisoner.
But thou, at least, art left some little cheer,
    Since from the passless portals of thy daughter

Thou canst her gentle, pious accents hear,
    While blinded I by floods of bitterest water
Rush to that marble where my angel lies,
And knock, and knock, and knock,—but none
    replies.

ADAPTED FROM THE ITALIAN OF VITORELLI.

AFTER the ball-room's glare,
    And fever, what delight
To breathe this balmy air,
    And view the chaften'd light,
Which o'er the clear ferene
    The fky's fair regent throws;
How tranquil is the fcene,
    What filence, what repofe!

No gadding zephyr breathes
    Among the branching firs,
Amid the feftoon'd wreaths
    Not even a leaflet ftirs:

The nightingale alone
  From bough to bough doth move,
And in a plaintive tone
  Calls to his abſent love.

She, ſtartled at his cries,
  Quick as ſhe can, draws near,
And lovingly replies,
  "Ah, weep not! I am here."
What tender troth they vow,
  Their ſighs how ſoft they be;
Why, Mary, wilt not thou
  Make ſuch reſponſe to me?

QUANDO ELPIN.

F. ROMANI.

HEN Elpin, weeping, perseveres
    To supplicate thy love, thy ruth,
Place not too much belief in tears,
    For they but seldom tell the truth.

With one benignant glance thou mayst
    Thy lover's martyrdom console,
But let the glance thou giv'st be chaste,
    His bold assurance to control.

It may be he requeſt a ſmile,
   One little ſmile do not deny;
But let him ſee thee coy the while,
   Nor with another ſmile reply.

But if he ſhould a kiſs demand,
   One kiſs alone and nothing more;
That, Roſe, with all thy ſtrength withſtand,
   The kiſs beſtow'd,—all, all is o'er.

Thou know'ſt not what fierce fire it wakes,
   What poiſon the ſweet lips convey,
It adds freſh force to him who takes,
   From her who gives takes all away.

When maiden yielding to its flames
   For the firſt time her love has kiſt,
"Give all the reſt," the heart exclaims,
   And ſhe's too feeble to reſiſt.

ALFIERI.

HAT! here in this neglected tomb remain
　　The bones of the great epic bard, who sole
Made the antique trump resound in modern strain,
　　And echo through the world from pole to pole?
What!—Rome a monument to him deny
　　Who soar'd to heaven upon immortal wings,
While here, in this your greatest temple, lie
　　The wretched rabble of your bishop-kings?
Ye swarms of dead that never were alive,
　　Arise! begone! and let the Vatican

Be purged from the foul smells that still sur-
    vive,
  And in its fairest midst be placed a man.
There were a shrine sole worthy of the two,
To Tasso raised by Michael Angelo.

SONNET AFFIXED TO THE PORTAL OF

ST. PETER'S, ROME.

March 10, 1861.

HEN the pale judge to abject terror prey,
   To his propofal bade the mob reply,
In their black rancour unrelenting they
   Cried "Live Barabbas, and let Jefus die!"
He died—borne down by the difgrace and pain,
   And was beholden hanging from the tree,
But the third day triumphant rofe again,
   Crown'd with the palms of his new victory.
Drunkards, perceiving not their fin's extent,

Pius! prefer a robber unto thee,
And in their madness are most confident.
But as God-man invincible thou'lt see,
Phœnix-like rising, at thy feet fall down
Him who now dares to snatch away thy crown.

The Following Three Pieces are from
Professor Severini's rendering of
the original Japanese.

THE lilies on Cogava's brink
    Tofs their fair heads on high,
While low their shadow-sisters sink,
    Of their own beauty shy.
Ah! why as when a child, ah, why
    Can I not wet my sleeve with the certainty
Of gathering those which at the bottom lie?

The bird of song in Naniva
Her home of plum-flowers forms,
But by her tears
Betrays her fears

Lest they be swept away
By desolating storms.
But to preserve unharm'd those flowers,
Could tender tears avail,
Dost think I'd weep less plenteous showers
Than thou, poor Nightingale!

Where is the realm of the wind,
The flowers' implacable foe?
For I would forth to encounter it. But no,
Blest rather are ye flowers that find
Death sweet, disperse and disappear;
Man has on earth a long career,
But where's the thing, whatever be its span,
Whose end is half so sad as that of man?

Florence, 1877.

www.ingramcontent.com/pod-product-compliance
Lightning Source LLC
Chambersburg PA
CBHW032135160426
43197CB00008B/650